AF207565

FREE ENTERPRISE ECONOMICS
IN AMERICA

Tom Rose

American Enterprise Publications
Mercer, PA 16137-3827

American Enterprise Publications
177 N. Spring Road
Mercer, Pennsylvania 16137
724-748-3726
www.biblicaleconomics.com

Copyright ©2002 by Tom Rose
All rights reserved.
Second Printing 2003
Third Printing 2004
Fourth Printing 2006
Fifth Printing 2008

No part of this publication may be reproduced, stored in a retrieval system, or transmitted, in any form or by any means, electronic, mechanical, photocopying, recording, or otherwise, without the prior written permission of the publisher.

Scripture taken from the King James version.

ISBN 0–9612198-9-0
Library of Congress Control Number 2002091435

Cover design by Wayne Rongaus, Rongaus Design
Printed in the United States of America

My deepest thanks to Ruth, my wife and partner in life, for her dedicated work as editor and helpful critic in publishing this work.

Contents

PREFACE

The historic free enterprise system in America is much more than just a system of applied economic science. It has a moral foundation that is solidly based on the Christian theology of the Bible. It is important that teachers and students appreciate this biblical foundation if they are to truly understand the essence of American freedom that created the beneficial political and economic climate that gave birth to what we call the system of free enterprise economics.

The previous booklet, which this new publication replaces, went through many, many printings over more than a quarter of a century. Its original purpose was to provide teachers in Christian schools and colleges, as well as parents who home school, with some key concepts about the historic American system of voluntary exchange, which quickly became the wonder of the world. The goal of this new publication remains the same, but it has been thoroughly updated and extensively revised to be even more helpful in communicating the spiritual, political, and economic basis of America's freedom to upcoming generations.

It is the principle of voluntary exchange between free individuals who stand self-responsible before their Creator, the God of the Bible, which was, and still remains, the true essence of the wonderfully productive economic system that we call free enterprise economics. Without the theology of the Bible free enterprise economics would never have evolved in

America, nor will it ever take root and prosper in any other country in the absence of its biblical roots. If this system of morally based exchange is to survive in America during this age of increasing secular humanism, its workings and underlying biblical principles must be effectively communicated to each upcoming generation.

The reason why some concepts found in this booklet deal with the moral foundations of the American system is to counterbalance the humanistic presentation of so-called "purely scientific" economics which is generally taught in America's tax-supported schools and universities. Thus, we boldly present the American free enterprise system of economics from a biblical perspective.

Other concepts deal with the practical economic functioning of our system, as well as with some of the ever-growing interventions by civil government which adversely affect the workings of what would otherwise be a pure free-market economy. The concepts presented in this booklet have been used during many years of successful teaching. Many ideas have also been excerpted from publications and articles I have authored, some of which are listed on the back cover of this publication.

After numerous reprints it is time to update and republish **FREE ENTERPRISE ECONOMICS** under its new title, **FREE ENTERPRISE ECONOMICS IN AMERICA**. It is our hope that you will find the ideas and insights in this new publication both thought provoking and stimulating. Finally, it is our hope that you will find it useful as a means of building God's Kingdom here on earth by reconstructing the foundations of our American Republic as we await the coming of our Lord and Master, Jesus Christ; for it is Him whom we serve as we engage in voluntary and mutually beneficial economic exchange with our fellowmen, both domestically and internationally.

Tom Rose

CHAPTER 1

GOD: The Author of Liberty

In the beginning God . . .
– Genesis 1:1

If the ideal of freedom is to be preserved in any nation, its people must first understand the biblical philosophy of freedom. Unless a people understand this unique philosophy of freedom upon which truly free political/economic systems and social institutions are based, they will be unable to defend it effectively. Those who carelessly take freedom for granted and do not recognize the need to defend it on a daily basis are already well on the way to losing it. For this reason parents and teachers have a key role, and a grave responsibility, in working to preserve liberty for the next generation.

The great Irish patriot and judge, John Philpot Curran (1750-1817), gave this warning to his own countrymen:

> It is the common fate of the indolent to see their rights become a prey to the active. The condition upon which God hath given liberty to man is eternal vigilance; which condition if he break, servitude is at once the consequence of his crime and the punishment of his guilt.

Does not Curran's warning apply equally well to free men everywhere? An unknown author admonishes in a similar vein:

To be born a free man is an accident;
To live as one is a responsibility;
To die free is an obligation.

The American free enterprise system, which is generally called the free-market system, can best be defined very simply as the voluntary exchange of goods and services between free and self-responsible individuals. Note that true freedom cannot be separated from one's self-responsibility before God. Freedom is not simply license to do anything we wish; rather, true freedom is closely tied to our responsibility to serve God.

It is important to note that our historic system of free enterprise economics is much more than just an economic system. The concept of free (i.e., voluntary) exchange between individuals which is inherent in the American system rests on a philosophical base that is theological at heart. So those who would understand the system and its underlying philosophy must also understand its theological base. Without that understanding there can be no real appreciation for self-responsible freedom.

Why should man be free? For an answer to this question we can look to Moses as he stood before Pharaoh and cried, "Thus saith the Lord, 'Let my people go that they may serve me'" (Ex. 8:1). The fact that our ancestors came to the New World to find religious liberty is so generally accepted as to need no explanation. Then why not go the extra step and acknowledge that man *must* be free and self-responsible so that he may serve his Creator?

The American system of free enterprise developed from two biblical precepts:

1) That man has a *right to be free* because he is created in the very image and likeness of God. ". . . Let us make man in our image, after our likeness: . . . " (Gen.1:26); and

2) That man has a *duty to maintain his freedom* so that he can serve his Lord and Creator (Ex. 8:1).

The economic application we make from these biblically revealed truths is that man is created a free being and is thereby capable of making value judgments, just like God does. Man, because he is made in God's very image, is capable of making decisions for which he, and he alone, is responsible. This is what self-responsibility is all about. Man has the ability, just like God, to impute value onto things and to make choices based on his earlier value imputations. In short, man can look at something and think, "In my opinion, item #1 is worth more than item #2." He thereby ranks his choices according to an internal, subjective scale of value that is unique to himself alone. This explains why man's right to individual action must be protected, else he can be robbed of his self-responsibility before God. And to do this would be to turn man into a chattel. Without man's God-given ability to impute (i.e., place) value onto things and upon the choices that are open to him, there could be no science of Economics, which is simply the study of how man imputes value onto things and on his available options.

Each person, standing as a free and self-responsible creature before his Creator, is designed by God to have, not only the mental ability to compute and arrange his own unique internal subjective scale of values, but also to have the social freedom to act externally upon those inner value imputations. And if we are to live in a free and voluntary society, each person has a duty to allow others to enjoy the same God-given internal and external freedom that he enjoys. The principle to be practiced is, "Do unto others as you would have them do unto you," the so-called "Golden Rule." This is the inherent morality of the free-market system. For instance, for me to force others to abide by my own unique internal value judgments is for me to deny them, not only their God-given *right* to be self-directing individuals, but also to deny them their God-given *responsibility* to answer to Him for the choices they make. It would be to dehumanize them, to animalize them by robbing them of their God-given freedom; in short, it would be to make them into chattel by turning them into something to be manipulated for my own purposes. This is what humanistically oriented (i.e., lawless) civil rulers and lawless individuals do when they arrogate unbiblical and unconstitutional powers to themselves.

> . . . The right to freedom being a gift of God Almighty, it is not in the power of man to alienate this gift and voluntarily become a slave.
> – Samuel Adams

> . . . a wise and frugal Government, which shall restrain men from injuring one another, shall leave them otherwise free to regulate their own pursuits of industry and improvement, and shall not take from the mouth of labor the bread it has earned. This is the sum of good government, . . .
> – Thomas Jefferson,
> in his first Inaugural Address, 1801

> God grants liberty only to those who love it, and are always ready to guard and defend it.
> – Daniel Webster

The free market system derives its inherent morality from man's created status as a free and self-responsible being before God. The voluntary exchange of goods and services between free and self-responsible individuals is the natural expression of biblical principles in economic terms. The moral defense of freedom of exchange in the marketplace can be stated in a negative way like this: Forced exchange is immoral because the one who applies force in wresting property from another robs that person of his rightfully acquired wealth. Thus, the applier of force is actually guilty of usurping the other person's God-given right and duty to be self-responsible before God for control of his wealth.

Use the Bible to teach economics? Why not? The Bible – God's revelation to man – is the long-recognized historical base of America's Christian heritage. It provides an important philosophical and theological defense of personal freedom, including economic freedom in the voluntary exchange of goods and services. All who object to this use of the Bible only show their ignorance of American history. They should be rescued from such ignorance.

One foreigner came to America as an objective observer in the 1830s to discover the secret of America's dynamic economic growth that was astounding all of Europe. He wrote:

> The Americans combine the notions of Christianity and of liberty so intimately in their minds that it is impossible to make them conceive the one without the other; and with them this conviction does not spring from that barren, traditionary faith which seems to vegetate rather than to live in the soul.
> – Alexis de Tocqueville

> . . . Despotism may govern without faith, but liberty cannot. Religion is much more necessary in the republic which they set forth in glowing colors, than in the monarchy which they attack; and it is more needed in democratic republics than in any others. How is it possible that society should escape destruction if the moral tie be not strengthened in proportion as the political tie is relaxed? and what can be done with a people which is its own master, if it be not submissive to the Divinity?
> – Alexis de Tocqueville

> . . . where the Spirit of the Lord is, there is liberty.
> – II Corinthians 3:17

CHAPTER 2

CIVIL GOVERNMENT: A Distributor of Higher Law

Give the king thy judgments, O God . . .
    – Psalm 72:1

If Americans value liberty, if they value freedom and self-responsibility before God as a desirable and moral state of affairs, then civil government will come to play a very minor role in their lives. Its role will then be limited to only being a protector of life and property and a punisher of those who physically harm or rob, steal, and cheat others. And as protector of man's God-given right to be free, the civil authority will not regulate and control but, rather, it will only serve as a revenger to execute wrath upon wrongdoers *after* the fact; for *prior* regulation is in itself a denial of freedom.

If, on the other hand, Americans come to fear the self-responsibility that is required by liberty, if they attempt to escape from the self-responsibility which is inherent in the free market system, then civil government will come to play an ever-increasing role in their lives. Instead of being simply a humble servant and protector of life and property, civil government will then become an arrogant and dictatorial regulator and master of the people, as well as a voracious re-distributor of the people's wealth. In short, government-mandated rules and regulations will invade every aspect of people's lives; no place of privacy will remain; and the civil authority will forcibly take wealth and income from some citizens and give it to other citizens who are politically favored.

To which role is civil government tending today? That of a humble and impartial protector of life, liberty, and property, or that of an arrogant regulator and voracious re-distributor of the people's wealth and income? Perhaps the burning issue of our day is: "What is the proper role of civil government in a free society?" How people answer this crucially important question will predetermine the degree of individual freedom and self-responsibility they will enjoy while living on this earth.

This question is also important in teaching about the free enterprise system of economics, for economic systems do not develop in a vacuum. Economic systems take root and develop in an atmosphere or environment which is greatly influenced by the existing political system of a country. The political system, in turn, is a product of a people's ruling political philosophy. And a nation's political philosophy is, in turn, a result of people's philosophy or view of man – what his origin is, what his purpose in life is, and what his destiny is. And, finally, a people's philosophy or view of man is directly a result of their theology or view of God. This relationship, starting with man's view of God (his theology) can be graphically shown as a pyramid:

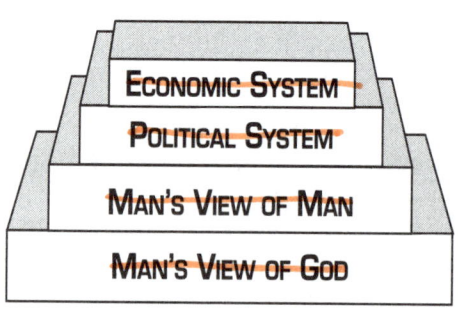

ECONOMIC SYSTEM

POLITICAL SYSTEM

MAN'S VIEW OF MAN

MAN'S VIEW OF GOD

Let us first summarize the essential relationship of the pyramidal diagram shown above, then we will discuss it more fully: A biblical view of God (biblical theology) will produce a biblical view of man (a world-and-life view, or philosophy of life, that is in harmony with God's revealed truth). A nation in which a biblical view of man is dominant will naturally produce a political system which protects and preserves the individual's God-given right to be free and self-responsible. And in such a morally wholesome social environment of freedom, it is only natural for a voluntary system of free economic exchange to evolve. This gives a brief summation of what developed in the history of these United States of America – a free society and a free market economy was the ultimate fruit of a people who had a biblical view of God and man.

Let us now review another cause-effect relationship: An unbiblical view of God will certainly produce an unbiblical view of man (a humanistic view in which man attempts to usurp the role of God as King of kings and Ruler of the universe). This will naturally lead to some form of tyrannical political rule through which the people will be subjugated. And in the resulting lack of individual freedom and self-responsibility, some form of totalitarian economic system will develop (socialism, fascism, or communism). This is a brief summation of how most non-free systems developed in most of the world.

In totalitarian countries civil government tends to be viewed as the source of law, and sometimes even as the voice of the people. In some countries the people tend to view civil government and society, incorrectly, as one and the same.

You probably have heard the following statement, even in our own country, by persons who do not understand the biblical relationship between God, man, and civil government: "Government? Why, 'We the People' *are* the government!" Such a statement is erroneous because biblical civil government is simply a social agency with limited powers set up by the people to preserve godly law and order.

In Western countries, and especially in America which has a strong Christian heritage, the people have historically held a biblical view of civil government. Therefore, they look upon civil rulers (the king, the emperor, the president, or the prime minister) simply as God's servants who are appointed to be distributors of God's higher law. Civil government is then correctly viewed as a God-appointed social agency for maintaining God's law and justice in a yet sinful and imperfect world. For example, when King Solomon at the young age of 20 ascended the throne upon his father's death, he prayed to God, "Give therefore thy servant an understanding heart to judge thy people, that I may discern between good and bad: for who is able to judge this thy so great a people?" (I Ki. 3:9). Solomon clearly understood the "Higher Law" principle: It is God who instituted the moral law of the universe.

Civil rulers are never the source of law – only God is the source of law. Therefore, the proper role of civil rulers is limited to discovering and discerning God's existing law (found in the Bible, and hopefully in each nation's political constitution) and to faithfully administer such law among the people, who belong to God and not to the king. In short, citizens are not just servile subjects of the king or other civil rulers who sometimes claim to have unlimited authority over the people. Rather, in a properly discerned civil government, the political rulers are simply God's servants who have been entrusted with the important responsibility of preserving the peace so the people will be free to serve God to the best of their individual abilities (Deut.17:14-20; Ex. 8:1, 18:13-26). This point is so important that it needs to be stated again: The only proper role of civil rulers is to search out and to apply God's higher law impartially to society; this is the *only* God-appointed role and duty of civil rulers. Any assumed role beyond God's limited assignment of power is sure to lead to some form of tyranny and thus to the loss of the people's freedom and self-responsibility.

Even rulers in nations with non-biblical heritages have recognized the fact that civil rulers are not a source of law but only distributors of higher law. Solon, a democratic ruler in Greece (638-559 B.C.), said, "A well constituted state is when the people obey the rulers, and the rulers obey the law."

The historic tendency of the state to become an active re-distributor of the people's wealth instead of only a defensive protector of their lives and property has brought forth some acid comments. Voltaire (1694-1778) charged, "The state is a device for taking money from one set of pockets and putting it into another." The American editor, author, and critic, H. L. Mencken (1880-1956) quipped in *A Carnival of Buncombe*, "Government is a broker in pillage, and every election is a sort of advance auction of stolen goods."

But in spite of some deservedly acid comments, most men would agree that civil government, properly constituted (Ah, that is the issue!), is both necessary and beneficial for the functioning of a free society. The Bible teaches that man's heart is evil: he will rob, cheat, and plunder his fellowmen if he can do so with impunity. "The heart is deceitful above all things, and desperately wicked: who can know it?" (Jer.17:9). A free society (and even an unfree one) needs some force that will restrain and punish evildoers. "If men were angels," said James Madison (1751-1836), "no government would be necessary. . . . "

So, civil government is necessary because evil abounds in the hearts and minds of individuals, even in the hearts and minds of civil rulers! Thus, we must also recognize what kind of "animal" civil government is, lest it be put to a wrong use. A farmer, after all, does not hitch a rooster to a plow. No, when he wants to plow a field he hitches up an ox or his old Missouri mule. Certain animals have capabilities that make them fit to do certain kinds of work. This truth should be kept in mind when the people of a country determine what powers can safely be delegated to and placed on the "animal" called civil government.

When the Articles of Confederation were being considered, the town of West Springfield, Massachusetts, recognized what kind of "animal" civil government is. In 1778 the Town Council gave these instructions to its representatives concerning the "weakness of human nature and the growing thirst for power."

It is *freedom*, Gentlemen, it is *freedom* & not a choice of the *forms of servitude* for which we contend, . . . We entertain no jealousy of the present Congress but who knows but in some future corrupt times there may be a Congress which will form a design upon the liberties of the People & will it be difficult to execute such a design when they have the absolute command of the navy, the army, & the purse?

An old French proverb also recognizes what kind of "animal" civil government is: "Government is a watchdog to be fed, not a cow to be milked." The important question, then, is not whether we should have civil government or not, but *what role* it should play in society. How people answer the question "What is the proper role of civil government in society?" will determine whether they will live as a free people or as slaves. In a country blessed with a truly free market system, civil government is simply a protector of individual freedom rather than a feeder and caretaker of the people. Whenever the power of civil government is used to infringe upon rather than to protect the individual right to life, liberty, and property, its power is misdirected towards destructive ends and thereby enslaves the people.

That the sole object and only legitimate end of government is to protect the citizen in the enjoyment of life, liberty and property, and when the government assumes other functions it is usurpation and oppression.
– The Constitution of Alabama,
Article 1, Section 35

CHAPTER 3

AMERICA: Founded as a Christian Nation

Blessed is the nation whose God is the Lord . . .
– Psalm 33:12

No objective student of American history can deny that America's roots as a nation are solidly Christian. These roots are found both on this side of the ocean – in our founding documents and in the constitutions of the original thirteen States – and on the European continent. John Locke's influence on the founding fathers of these United States is still widely recognized today. What is generally overlooked today, though, is the fact that his influence was also solidly Christian. Locke's treatises on civil government abound with Christian ideas and biblical references. The same holds true to a lesser degree for other scholars of the European Enlightenment.

The Pilgrims who came to our shores in 1620 brought with them a rich Christian heritage which had great influence on the form of civil government that was incorporated into the state and national constitutions of these United States of America. Through the Mayflower Compact the Pilgrims covenanted with each other to establish a self-governing "civill Body Politick" with the specific objective of establishing a Christian covenant community in America similar to the self-governing republic established by the Israelites in the Old Testament. This biblical influence, along with that of the earlier Jamestown settlement in Virginia, solidly established the theological foundation for the American Republic.

Our founding fathers held life, liberty, and property to be God's gifts to man. During the Revolutionary War it was common practice for the Continental Congress to hold a day of prayer to invoke Divine assistance from the God who controls the destiny of men and nations. The Continental Congress also ordered 20,000 Bibles to be printed and distributed throughout the nation during the Revolutionary War. The need to follow Christian principles was emphasized even in the military:

> The General hopes and trusts, that every officer and man, will endeavor so to live, and act, as becomes a Christian Soldier defending the dearest Rights and Liberties of his country.
>
> – George Washington,
> General Order of July 9, 1776

These were not acts of Deists (men who believe in a god who created the universe, set it in motion, and then abandoned it to run all by itself). Rather, these were acts by men of deep faith who believed in the covenant God of the Bible.

Article 1, Section 7, of the Constitution of the United States of America explicitly states "Sundays excepted" in outlining when a bill passed by the Congress becomes a law without the President's signature. Finally, the U.S. Supreme Court unanimously declared on February 29, 1892, in the case of *Church of the Holy Trinity v. United States,* 143 U.S. 457 (1892), ". . . this is a Christian nation." Along with this famous declaration, the U.S. Supreme Court listed a whole series of historical instances to support their claim.

The founders of this nation were well-educated scholars. They were well acquainted with and understood the lessons of history. The Pilgrims were intimately familiar with their Bible. They understood the biblical concept of the separation of powers in civil government as found in Isaiah 33:22: "For the Lord is our judge (Judicial Department), the Lord is our lawgiver (Legislative Department), the Lord is our king (Executive Department); he will save us." (Material in parentheses added by author.) Here Isaiah expresses the theological concept of the division of governmental power to prevent tyranny that we find incorporated on a horizontal (departmental) basis in the Constitution of the United States of America. It is also found on a vertical basis in the division of civil power between our federal, state, and local governments.

Our forefathers thought biblically and faithfully applied biblical precepts to the institution of civil government. If we hope to preserve the biblically based free nation of limited government that they bequeathed us, then we must emulate them today by evaluating every aspect of civil government according to biblical precepts.

The principle of dividing civil government into vertical spheres is also found in Jethro's counsel to Moses about how to establish a good system of civil government after the Israelites fled Egypt:

> Moreover thou shalt provide out of all the people able men, such as fear God, men of truth, hating covetousness; and place such over them, to be rulers of thousands, and rulers of hundreds, rulers of fifties, and rulers of tens.
> – Exodus 18:21.

Note especially the high standard of character qualifications that God's people are to use as measuring sticks when choosing civil rulers to hold public office: able men who fear God; men of truth who hate covetousness. Such is the basis of the American ideal for local self-rule and the division of governing powers at the local, state and national levels. How many of our elected officials today meet these high standards? Will the covenant God of the Bible fail to judge a nation that deviates from applying the specific qualifications He gave us for choosing elected officials? Following God's standards leads to a biblical system of limited government with maximum freedom and self-responsibility being enjoyed by the people. On the other hand, failure to do so leads to centralized tyranny and the sure loss of freedom.

Another testimony to America's Christian roots is the fact that all of our early institutions of higher learning in America made specific reference to Jesus Christ. Take, for instance, the Rules and Precepts of Harvard College of 1642:

> Let every Student be plainly instructed, and earnestly pressed to consider well, the maine end of his life and studies is, to know God and Jesus Christ which is eternall life, John 17:3 and therefore to lay Christ in the bottome, as the only foundation of all sound knowledge and Learning.

The current denial and denigration of America's Christian heritage in removing all reference to God pertaining to civil government, and in our schools of learning, is a contemporary aberration which serves to undermine and eventually destroy the historic Christian influence that is the essence of America's character and greatness.

> Then shalt thou call, and the Lord shall answer; . . . Here I am. . . .
> And the Lord shall guide thee continually, and satisfy thy soul in drought, and make fat thy bones: and thou shalt be like a watered garden, and like a spring of water, whose waters fail not.
>
> – Isaiah 58:9 &11

CHAPTER 4

PROPERTY: The Economic Basis of Individual Freedom and Self-Responsibility

Is it not lawful for me to do what I will with mine own?
– Matthew 20:15

The idea of property is to have an exclusive ownership right in something; that is, to own, control, enjoy, and even to dispose of it as your very own without giving any explanation or reason to anyone else, even to the civil authority. But the concept of property runs deeper than most people think, penetrating to a person's very inner moral fiber or soul. The "something" that you own, at its most basic level, is your mind and physical body, as well as the wealth that you create through your mental and physical effort. In actuality, a property right or ownership is based on the legal relationship that exists between a person's inner being (soul) and his mind and body and the outward physical things he owns. Not only does a person have a property right to the physical wealth he has either produced or has honestly acquired by expending his mental or physical effort, but each person also has a property in his own being or self. That is, each person has a precious and exclusive property right to his thoughts, opinions, attitudes, and product of his own efforts. He has the sole moral and legal right to direct and control his labor power (both mental and physical), and he alone has the moral and legal right to claim undisputed ownership of the fruit of his labor.

Note that we have stated the concept of property in various ways to assure full understanding. The reason for doing this is because a correct understanding of property or ownership is crucial to one's understanding of his personal responsibility before God. God created the universe, then He created man. Therefore, as Creator, God has complete and unquestioned ownership and control of the whole universe as well as of man. He can mold man and the universe as He sees fit. Since man is created in the very image and likeness of God, he shares some of God's attributes. One aspect of man's sharing God's attributes is his right to property and control over his own thoughts, words, actions, and production of wealth, all of which are to be done to the honor and glory of God as man's Creator. Without this God-given property right, man cannot be free and independent of outside influences which might otherwise impose control over him. Even more importantly, without an exclusive right of property in his own being and product of his own labor, man cannot be wholly self-responsible to God.

The right to property is an inherent right bestowed by God; it predates the existence of the State. And civil rulers have a God-appointed duty to protect the individual's right to property to the exclusion of anyone else.

Noah Webster, in his first edition of *An American Dictionary of the English Language* of 1828 defines property as:

> The exclusive right of possessing, enjoying and disposing of a thing; ownership. In the beginning of the world, the Creator gave to man dominion over the earth, over the fish of the sea and the fowls of the air, and over every living thing. This is the foundation of man's *property* in the earth and in all its productions. Prior occupancy of land and of wild animals gives to the possessor the *property* of them. The labor of inventing, making or

producing any thing constitutes one of the highest and most indefeasible titles to *property*. *Property* is also acquired by inheritance, by gift or by purchase. *Property* is sometimes held in common, yet each man's right to his share in common land or stock is exclusively his own.

Webster's discussion of *Literary property* sheds additional light on the important topic of property:

> *Literary property*, the exclusive right of printing, publishing and making profit by one's own writings. No right or title to a thing can be so perfect as that which is created by a man's own labor and invention. The exclusive right of a man to his literary productions, and to the use of them for his own profit, is entire and perfect, as the faculties employed and labor bestowed are entirely and perfectly his own. On what principle then can a legislature or a court determine that an author can enjoy only a *temporary property* in his own productions? If a man's right to his own *productions in writing* is as perfect as to the *productions* of his farm or his shop, how can the former be abridged or limited, while the latter is held without limitation? Why do the *productions* of *manual labor* rank higher in the scale of rights or *property*, than the *productions* of the *intellect*?

James Madison, who played such a major role in the writing of the Constitution of these United States of America, classified property as external and internal. He said external property is "a man's land, merchandize, or money." He regarded internal property as man's

> . . . opinions and the free communication of them.
>
> He has a property of peculiar value in his religious opinions, and in the profession and practice dictated by them.

. . . He has an equal property in the free use of his faculties and free choice of the objects on which to employ them.

. . . Conscience is the most sacred of all property; . . .

John Locke pointed out in his *Of Civil Government* that man's property in himself stems from man's being God's property:

> . . . and Reason, which is that Law {i.e., the Law of Nature}, teaches all Mankind, who will but consult it; That being all equal and independent, no one ought to harm another in his Life, Health, Liberty or Possessions; for Men being all the Workmanship of one Omnipotent, and infinitely wise Maker; All the Servants of one Sovereign Master, sent into the World by his order and about his business, they are his Property, whose Workmanship they are, . . . (Here Locke paraphrases Eph. 2:10.)

It is this essential concept of property that a person must grasp before he can understand the spirit and essence of the idea of free enterprise, which is defined as the voluntary exchange of goods and services between free and self-responsible individuals. Each man must, if he is to be responsible for himself before God, have a full property in himself and in the fruit of his labor. In no other way can a person be responsible to God for every thought, word, and action – which is what self-responsibility is all about. Psalm 24:1 states, "The earth is the Lord's, and the fullness thereof; the world, and they that dwell therein."

The original American idea of property is taken from the biblical idea of property: that man holds property in trusteeship to God while he is living on this earth, and that man is directly responsible to God, and only indirectly responsible to his fellowmen, for the use he makes of his property. Mark Hopkins (1868) showed another aspect concerning the inherent morality of private ownership and control of wealth: "The acquisition of property is required by love because it is a powerful means of benefitting others."

The science of economics could not exist if we did not beforehand recognize the moral right to property. The study of economics, in its most essential form, rests on man's right to have discretionary control over himself and the wealth he produces. In short, the whole science of economics ultimately rests on man's God-given right to have property in himself, that is, for man to have both the right and responsibility to use his mental and physical faculties as well as his wealth in the service of his Creator.

There is not a single instance in history, in which civil liberty was lost, and religious liberty preserved entire. If therefore we yield up our temporal property, we at the same time deliver the conscience into bondage.

– John Witherspoon

CHAPTER 5

VOLUNTARISM: The Crucial Element in Free Exchange

> But without thy mind would I do nothing.
> – Philemon 14

Some people genuinely fear the idea of free enterprise because they erroneously envision the "weak" being oppressed by the "strong." Most who favor the ideas of socialism/communism hold this mistaken view of the free market system. Such a view is expressed by J. K. Galbraith in *Economics and the Public Purpose*: "Left to themselves, economic forces do not work out for the best except perhaps for the most powerful."

Galbraith's view overlooks one pivotal point about the free-market economy. That is, if the civil government plays its proper role in society as a guarantor of peaceful exchange, then no one, regardless of how powerful he might be, is capable of applying coercive force on anyone else. In short, any coerced exchange is *not* a free exchange; thus it is *outside of and alien to* the very concept of free exchange that is found in the free enterprise system.

And this brings us to an important point to consider, but not in the way that Galbraith means: It is true that strong and influential individuals or parties in society sometimes use their influence to induce the civil authority to institute legislation and to make rules and regulations that favor the strong over the weak. But this is not the kind of free enterprise that exists in a politically free society. Rather it is the kind of government favoritism that naturally occurs under socialism, communism, or fascism – all types of totalitarian societies.

Civil rulers seem to have a natural inclination to gradually arrogate more power to themselves under the guise of "protecting the public." The end result is a myriad of government-control agencies which minutely regulate an increasing number of economic exchanges which individuals previously could freely offer to each other for their mutual benefit. Licensing boards proliferate, and government agencies regulate and/or prohibit the buying and selling of many products and services which politicians and their bureaucrats deem the general public too ignorant to consume without government consent and supervision.

Gradually, the populace forget their prior freedom and consider their new regulated status quo to be normal. Johann Wolfgang von Goethe (1749-1832) stated, "None are more hopelessly enslaved than those who falsely believe they are free."

Coercive exchanges that do take place in society cannot be corrected by eliminating freedom in the marketplace. They can only be corrected by eliminating the *condition* that allows forced exchange to occur in the first place. Without exception, the cause of coercive (unfree) exchanges will be found to be either:

1) that the civil authorities, who are the sole source of any lasting monopoly power in society, provide special protection for favored parties against would-be competitors, or

2) that government officials "wink their eye" when some favored entity in the economy exerts illegal force on others in society.

Both of these deviations from free exchange are induced by civil rulers who fail to impartially apply the rule of law to everyone in society. In short, lawless civil rulers make some entities in society "more equal" than others, thus "legal" coercion of the weak by the strong is the result. The solution is not to reduce people's scope of freedom, but to eliminate the abuse of political favoritism.

What we are saying is this: Any malfunctioning of voluntarism in the economy will not be solved by moving *away from* the free market ideal through the imposition of government controls and interventions but, rather, by moving *towards* the free market ideal of voluntarism.

America's abortive experience with wage and price controls (August, 1971, to April, 1974) during the Nixon presidential administration serves as mute testimony to this fact. That disastrous experiment in government totalitarianism brought economic chaos by making many once-free exchanges illegal. The lesson learned was that government-induced, or government-allowed, impediments that stymie the practice of voluntary exchange must be found and rooted out. What is called for is a rigorous and impartial application of the same rule – the reign of voluntary free exchange – to every entity in society. In short, no government favoritism bestowed on anybody; everyone plays by the same rule! The application of such a rule will automatically produce a free-market economy. After all, what would we think of a hockey or baseball game in which the rules were unfairly twisted to favor one team over another?

The crucial role played by voluntarism in the free-market system is simply this: The rule of voluntarism guarantees that *both* parties to free economic exchange will benefit from the exchange, assuming that neither party errs in his judgment or calculations, which is always a possibility. But the possibility of honest error is a facet of free exchange that provides an opportunity to learn by experience. It is also demanded by the biblical principle of self-responsibility. A baby would never learn to walk without the freedom to fall down and get back up. Without the possibility of making occasional errors, individuals could never grow in experience, wisdom, and the practice of living as free persons – worse yet, they would be continually dependent upon the civil government to protect them!

> It is not the function of our Government to keep the citizen from falling into error; it is the function of the citizen to keep the Government from falling into error.
>
> – U.S. Supreme Court,
> *Communications Assn. v. Douds*, 339 U.S. 382 (1950)

And why does the reign of voluntarism guarantee that both parties to an exchange will benefit? Who, after all, would willingly enter into a one-sided bargain to his own detriment? For the answer to our question, just suppose that coercion reigned instead of voluntarism: The strong would then be free to tyrannize the weak and plunder them at will! The guarantee of voluntary exchange protects the poor and weak against the rich and strong by giving the poor person the option of saying to the rich person, "No, I don't want to trade with you unless you make it worth my while!" But if coercion rules, one party will quickly seize the opportunity to benefit at the other's expense.

Thomas Davidson emphasizes the inherent morality of voluntary (non-coercive) exchange that reigns in the free market economy with this observation:

> That which is not free is not responsible, and that which is not responsible is not moral.

The idea is clear: If each person is to stand as a self-responsible individual before his Creator, then both parties to an exchange must be free to negotiate voluntary exchanges and thereby personally benefit or suffer from the results of their free actions.

It is important to recognize that the reign of voluntarism actually prevents the powerful from oppressing the weak in a free-market economy. For instance, suppose that a powerful (rich?) man wants a weak (poor?) man to work for him (i.e., to cooperate economically). If voluntarism does indeed reign in society, then the rich man must somehow peacefully induce or persuade the poor man that it will be to his advantage to do so. And, as long as the poor man is free to refuse to cooperate (he might want to work for someone else, or even want to go fishing), then the rich man can gain the poor man's economic cooperation *only* by sharing a part of the expected fruits of his economic partnership with the poor man! If the law proscribes him from using force on his weaker fellowman, then the rich man has only one alternative: He must "sweeten the pot," so-to-speak, until he is able to gain the willing cooperation of the poor man. Only then will the poor man agree to cooperate voluntarily with the rich man.

In short, we now can see this truth clearly: Economic freedom, the reign of voluntary exchange between free and self-responsible individuals, actually helps the weak more than the powerful. Why is this so? Because in the absence of voluntarism, the rich man would be in a position to buy the assistance of coercive agents in society to apply force on the poor man. In the final analysis, the reign of voluntarism in the free enterprise system is the poor man's guarantee of getting a "fair shake" in the marketplace.

Before leaving the topic of voluntarism, it will be fruitful to take up again the viewpoint expressed by Mr. Galbraith that economic forces in the free market benefit the powerful at the expense of the less powerful. Mr. Galbraith favored the idea of having the civil government intervene in the marketplace to "protect" the common man. Actually, the federal government started doing this in the 1880s with the initiation of the Interstate Commerce Commission (ICC) to regulate railroad rates. More federal agencies were steadily added all during the twentieth century: the Federal Trade Commission (FTC), the Federal Communications Commission (FCC), the Federal Reserve System (FRS), the Environmental Protection Agency (EPA), the Drug Enforcement Agency (DEA), the Food and Drug Administration (FDA), and many others – in total, over 85 different control agencies!

Each of these government agencies, in one way or another, interferes with and impedes what would otherwise be true voluntary exchange in the marketplace. But something that the common man did not expect to happen occurred:

Big corporations, powerful financial groups, and special interests that always operate behind the scenes soon found ways to gain influence and effective control over the government agencies. Thus, it became a common practice to play the game of "musical chairs" in which business and financial executives move from business firms in the controlled industries to the controlling government agencies, and vice versa. So much for "protecting" the consumer! There is a name for such a system of government-control agencies, the name is *fascism* – a system in which government does not *own* but *effectively controls* the various economic entities. The *real* controllers, though, are not the government of the people, but rather the special-interest groups who have gained effective control over the government agencies!

Take, for instance, two government agencies as examples, the Federal Reserve System (FRS) and the Food and Drug Administration (FDA). Rather than protecting the purchasing value of the dollar, the FRS has long served as an "engine of monetary inflation" to really protect the inflationary lending policies of large banks at the expense of small banks and the general public. Since the Federal Reserve System was established in 1913, the dollar has lost over 95 percent of its purchasing power. In short, a dollar saved in 1913 and spent today would have a purchasing power of less than five cents!

The Food and Drug Administration (FDA) had its beginning in 1906 allegedly to "protect" the consumer, who was otherwise deemed incapable of looking out for his own interests in the marketplace. Today the FDA regulates approximately 25 percent of America's total yearly economic output – Gross National Product (GNP). It controls everything from food packaging and labeling to dictating what medicines and drugs consumers can and cannot purchase, as well as how medical practitioners must treat their patients. Critics of the FDA complain that it is manipulated and controlled by special-interest groups made up of large pharmaceutical companies and licensed medical practitioners who work together to push the use of chemicals and drugs to the exclusion of safe, non-toxic alternatives in the pursuit of health.

Recently, in a congressional hearing on Dr. Stanislaw Burzynski's harassment by the FDA, Rep. Richard M. Burr made the following statement:

The FDA's abuse of power transcends regulatory misconduct. It constitutes nothing less than one of the worst abuses of the criminal justice system I have ever witnessed.

At issue was Dr. Burzynski's method of curing cancer through his very effective antineoplaston approach. Hundreds and hundreds of the doctor's patients have been cured, and they have testified to that fact. But the FDA steadfastly refuses to let Dr. Burzynski conduct his successful practice in peace because his alternative method has not been officially approved by the FDA, which makes the spurious claim of being the sole authority capable of approving or disproving all medical practices. It is reported that, over a 12-year period, the FDA spent millions of taxpayers' dollars in an attempt to destroy Dr. Burzynski's antineoplaston approach to the cure of cancer.

The doctor has endured four grand juries, a criminal indictment of 15 charges that could have put him in jail for 85 years, and two jury trials (the last one ended in March, 1997). But Dr. Burzynski was decisively vindicated by the jurors in every instance.

Question: Why should the FDA conduct such vicious vendettas against alternative medical practitioners? Answer: The standard medical cancer cures (meaning the FDA-approved cures) all involve high-priced drugs and very expensive FDA- approved procedures such as surgery, radiation, and chemotherapy. Standard medical practitioners and the entire chemical/drug industry currently feast off of a multibillion dollar market that is carefully controlled by the FDA and the professional licensing authorities. Is it any wonder that special-interest groups will go to great extremes to protect the source of their lucrative incomes from outside competitors?

> . . . Demetrius . . .
>
> . . . called together . . . the workmen of like occupation, and said, Sirs, ye know that by this craft we have our wealth.
>
> . . . almost throughout all Asia, this Paul hath persuaded and turned away much people, saying that they be no gods, which are made with hands:
>
> So that . . . our craft is in danger to be set at nought; . . .
>
> – Acts 19:24-27

The question to be answered is this: Will the "poor" of this world – consumers in particular and citizens in general – be better protected by government oversight through a myriad of governmental control agencies, or by implementing the simple rule of voluntarism in the marketplace? The former route entails the continual maintenance of a very expensive government bureaucracy to which special-interest groups have ready access to stymie would-be competitors. The latter route simply entails a very limited civil government that is restricted to its God-given role of serving as ". . . a revenger to execute wrath upon him that doeth evil" (Rom.13:4).

> It is the theory of all modern civilized governments that they protect and foster the liberty of the citizen; it is the practice of all of them to limit its exercise, and sometimes very narrowly.
>
> – H. L. Mencken

CHAPTER 6

COMPETITION: The Assurance That Exchange Will Be Free

It is naught, it is naught, saith the buyer:
but when he is gone his way,
then he boasteth.
- Proverbs 20:14

We have seen that the reign of voluntarism in the market place provides assurance that both parties to an exchange will benefit. In truth, if one party or the other saw no benefit, he would quickly withdraw from the exchange. As long as the civil authority faithfully serves as an impartial protector of the peace, no one will be able to force his will upon another. But what economic force is at work in the free-market economy to assure that exchanges are indeed voluntary? That impartial force is competition. As long as a person has a choice open to him, he can then select the most rewarding alternative to suit his needs.

It is not necessary that the economist's textbook concept of "perfect competition" be in effect. It is not necessary that a buyer or seller have an infinite or even a large number of choices to select from. "Effective competition" (two or three available options) is generally sufficient to substantially lower buying prices on the one hand and to bid up selling prices on the other.

For instance, two people bidding against each other to purchase a used car is all that is needed to drive up the selling price. Likewise, two sellers who are anxious to do business are sufficient to drive prices down as they competitively cut their asking price to win the business of a customer from a competing seller. It is only in rare instances that the free-market economy will not provide at least that much effective competition. Usually there is substantially more. But if there isn't, in a truly free market a person is never forced to act because he always has the option of postponing a purchase or altering consumption while waiting for prices to fall. Sellers, on the other hand, also have an option. They can refrain from offering goods for sale in the hope that a more attractive price might appear later on. These are marginal decisions that are voluntarily arrived at by many widely dispersed individuals throughout the market economy, or by only one or two individuals in very small markets, but each individual decision contributes a meaningful impact on the outcome of prices in the marketplace.

In the automobile market there were sharp decreases in auto prices in 1957 (a recession period) and also in the prices of large autos in 1974 (because of the OPEC oil embargo). As this is being written today, auto prices have been decreasing once again (because of a looming recession after an inflationary bubble that lasted more than a decade). The price of fuel suddenly started to skyrocket in 2001 because of an alleged oil shortage. Once again motorists responded by imputing a lower value on gas-consuming SUVs and larger cars and switched to buying autos that gave improved gas mileage. These examples show how the marginal decisions of independently acting consumers quickly and dynamically raise or lower prices in the marketplace. Nothing sends a more powerful signal to entrepreneurs and merchants than the decisions of consumers to buy or not to buy.

A practical example of international competition at work in the auto industry, which benefitted consumers, occurred in the late 1980s when foreign auto manufacturers greatly increased their exports to America. Domestic American auto manufacturers responded by improving the quality of their autos and by meeting the challenge of lower-priced foreign imports. The result was a "buyers' market" which stimulated sales of both domestic and foreign cars. Consumers were pleased with a wider choice of selection, and the wages and profits of those engaged in domestic auto production rose.

The "rule of thumb" followed by the classical economists of the 1700s and 1800s was this: "If competition in the marketplace is absent or weak, then look to see what kind of governmental intervention might be inhibiting the free entry of profit-seeking entrepreneurs and workers." This is a wise approach to follow today, because profit-seeking entrepreneurs will always seek to compete in markets that are free of such interventions, and they will employ workers in the process. The resulting increase in supply provided by such entrepreneurs and their employees will quickly benefit consumers by driving prices downward; and lower prices will induce consumers to increase the quantity of goods and services they purchase. Everyone wins. The vast increase in the use of business and personal computers since the early 1980s is a perfect example of how free competition and open markets benefit everyone in the economy as prices fall. Today desktop computers are much lower in price, and much improved in quality and power, than they were 20 years ago. This writer paid $7,000 for a good-quality computer in 1982; 20 years later a much better computer with multiple times the power of the 1982 computer cost less than $1,500.

Nineteenth-century liberals, who would be called free-market conservatives today, feared the monopoly-bestowing power of civil government much more than they feared private business firms that competed in the open marketplace. The power wielded by private monopolies is very feeble unless it is protected by civil government, which then acts as a policing power to exclude would-be competitors, thus benefitting the government-protected monopoly with a protected market in which it alone can sell goods or services, at the expense of higher prices to consumers. The nineteenth-century liberals recognized that freedom to enter and exit from markets imposes a very healthy discipline upon the entire business community. Of course, no one likes to be disciplined, especially high-placed individuals who head large corporations. In fact, one inescapable lesson of history is that demands on civil rulers to limit competition from other would-be providers of goods and services usually comes from large, influential business firms and professional groups that have influential political ties.

For instance, much current activity of the licensed medical profession and the Food and Drug Administration (FDA) is devoted to suppressing the availability of safe, non-toxic alternative health products and treatments which threaten the incomes of the involved special-interest groups. The excuse, or "false whiskers" worn in denying consumers freedom of choice, is always, "We must protect the public from 'quacks' and from their own ignorance." Beware of such claims because they are usually made by persons who are more interested in raising their own incomes rather than in protecting the welfare of the public!

One experience in governmental suppression of competition that had a drastic impact on America was the chartering of the East India Company by Queen Elizabeth in 1600. It was given monopoly control of goods (including tea) from India into England and into her various colonies. Can we believe that such monopoly control was meant to benefit consumers rather than the stockholders of the East India Company? Can we believe that the motivation of government controllers and the self-interest of political intriguers behind the throne have changed over the last 400 years? The American colonists didn't think so because they recognized that the East India Company was being used to impose higher costs and an unwanted tax on them – thus the "Boston Tea Party" in 1773.

In 1913 the U.S. Congress established the Federal Reserve Bank (FRB) which now has almost absolute control over America's entire financial system. Can we believe that such monopoly control is for the protection of the public in general rather than for the specific benefit of special-interest groups that have political access? The same question should be asked about every government-created control agency that limits free competition in the marketplace (ICC, FCC, FTC, FRB, FDIC, FDA, etc.).

Senator Benjamin Hill eloquently expressed his fear of government power in a debate on the U.S. Senate floor in 1878, long before our current number of federal control agencies reached its current level of over 85! He warned:

> . . . I do not dread these corporations as instruments of power to destroy this country, because there are a thousand agencies which can regulate, restrain, and control them; but there is a corporation we may all well dread. That corporation is the Federal Government. From the aggressions of this corporation there can be no safety, if it be allowed to go beyond the well-defined limits of its power. I dread nothing so much as the exercise of ungranted and doubtful powers by this Government. It is in my opinion the danger of dangers to the future of this country. Let us be sure we keep it always within its limits. If this great, ambitious, ever-growing corporation become oppressive, who shall check it? If it become wayward, who shall control it? If it become unjust, who shall trust it? As sentinels on the country's watch-tower, Senators, I beseech you watch and guard with sleepless dread that corporation which can make all property and rights, all States and people, and all liberty and hope its playthings in an hour, and its victims forever.

One critic of interventionist government alludes to the dangerous tendency today of Americans to put their trust in the arbitrary power of civil rulers rather than in the impartial working of the competitive marketplace:

> If one were to say that State-worship is the official religion of the United States today, one would be guilty of exaggeration. But not by much.
>
> Increasingly, Americans today look to the State as the supreme authority, the ultimate lawgiver,

the grantor of all rights and privileges, the cure for all ills, the solution to all problems, the source of all blessings, the guarantor of all security, even the arbiter of right and wrong. In return, the State increasingly demands of its citizens their absolute loyalty, their unquestioning obedience, and ever-growing portions of their wealth for sustenance.

– John Eidsmoe, from the foreword to the re-print of Thomas Cooley's 1880 book,
The General Principles of Constitutional Law of the USA

If there is one aspect of culture that bodes evil for con-tinuation of economic and political freedom in our American Republic, it is the increasing tendency of American citizens to seek economic security through government regulation and controls rather than through open competition in the market-place. For, interventionist civil government does indeed fos-ter the growth of monopolistic and arbitrary power to be wielded by hidden powers behind civil rulers (Eph. 6:12). On the other hand, competitive markets foster the decentraliza-tion of power and the expansion of freedom of exchange, both of which work for the benefit of the common man.

From the Conduct of our Church and the Sen-ate, we see how *absolutely requisite* it is, to con-tinually guard against Power; for, when once Bodies of Men, in authority, get Possession of, or become invested with, Property or Prerogative, whether it be by Intrigue, Mistake, or Chance, they scarcely ever relinquish their Claim, even if founded in Iniquity itself.

–Hugh Hughes, in a letter to Charles Tillinghast, March 7, 1787

Put not your trust in princes, nor in the son of man, in whom there is no help.

Happy is he that hath the God of Jacob for his help, whose hope is in the Lord his God:

–Psalm 146: 3&5

CHAPTER 7

CONSUMER SOVEREIGNTY: A Necessary Discipline for Producers

Let the righteous smite me; it shall be a kindness:
and let him reprove me; it shall be an excellent oil, . . .
Psalm 141: 5

Who is able to control the giant corporations except the government? Is there not a danger that monopolistic firms can produce what they choose at engineered prices, and then foist off their products onto a helpless public through high-pressure advertising?

Thus goes the socialist/communist attack against what they call the "imperialistic" American free-enterprise system. The erroneous suggestion inherent in such a question is that "Big Government" is needed to keep "Big Business" in check. In other words, they allege that without government controls, large business firms would take unfair advantage of the poor, unprotected consumer.

Let's evaluate the validity of such an attack by analyzing how the free-market system actually works:

First, we must recognize that all economic activity – which includes pre-production economic planning and the actual production process itself – begins with the wants of individual consumers and ends with the satisfaction of those wants. All economic activities occurring between business firms, such as the purchase of raw materials and supplies, are simply intermediate steps of production towards the ultimate satisfaction of consumer wants.

Second, we must also recognize that consumers are self-interested individuals who are guided primarily by a desire to satisfy their own unique wants with the least expenditure of their scarce time and resources. Note that the consumer does not act as a beneficent philanthropist in the marketplace. The buyer is not at all interested in how much an item costs to produce. Consumers could care less whether the seller makes a profit or loss on what he sells. The sole guide of the consumer is, "Can I buy an identical item or a close substitute somewhere else more cheaply?" In this respect, the consumer is completely self-interested or "selfish."

Such consumer self-interestedness is both wholesome and necessary for the operation of the free-market economy because it imposes a positive discipline on producers. Without the constant pressure of consumer self-interest to serve as a stern but beneficial discipline on them, producers would eventually become sloppy in their business operations and allow their costs of production to rise out of control. Consumers thus exert a systematic discipline on producers which they cannot escape in a free and competitive marketplace. This is not to say that producers enjoy the impartial discipline of consumer sovereignty; far from it, for who does enjoy being disciplined by others? But consumer discipline on producers is inherent in the functioning of a truly free-market system. This fact helps explain why business leaders often seek "protection" from civil government – in the form of subsidies, government controls of one sort or another, and market-controlling legislation – all to escape from the otherwise inescapable market-imposed discipline of consumer sovereignty.

Let us investigate the matter further: Since consumers are constantly searching for a "better buy," entrepreneurs and other producers regularly find themselves under a continual, and often irksome, pressure which irritatingly pushes them to work day and night for cost-saving efficiencies in their business operations. This is why bosses continually admonish and exhort workers to cut costs. The name of the game then becomes, "Let's see what we can do to operate more efficiently so we can underbid our competitors in pricing our products and/or in improving their quality, thereby winning more customers." The businessman who does so, earns hard-won profits for himself and, in the process, higher wages for his employees! He who doesn't will experience losses and will have to lay off his workers! Accordingly, successful response to the often unwelcome discipline of consumer sovereignty requires a high degree of cooperation between business management and workers, with the benefit of higher profits and higher wages accruing to both parties.

This brings us to a third important point, which is the recognition that producers – including both management and labor – are also guided by self-interest, just as consumers are. Producers are willing to undergo the often distasteful, but healthy, discipline of enduring consumer sovereignty because they can earn good incomes by doing so. Successful companies invariably have managers and workers who jointly recognize the fact that consumers are their ultimate employers, whose loyalty management and labor must first win and then retain by continued efficiency of operation and superior service provided.

Fourth, more needs to be said about the fact that no one really likes to be under discipline. Producers will always have a tendency to escape from the unpleasant discipline imposed by consumers who are always looking for cheaper prices and better quality products for the money they spend. The easiest escape route, of course, if open, is to seek help from the civil authorities. Thus, business leaders and labor union leaders often push for government subsidies or government-imposed: price controls, protective tariffs, import quotas, international trade agreements and regulations like those found through the establishment of the World Trade

Organization (WTO) and the North American Trade Agreement (NAFTA).

Farmers often appeal for price supports and special low-cost government-loan programs. Labor unions seek minimum wage laws and monopoly control over employers' supplies of labor. Professional persons and skilled craftsmen seek to limit the free entry of new practitioners through the imposition of licensing laws which serve to artificially raise the incomes of the licensed parties at the expense of consumers. All of the above are examples of anti-free-market (coercive) attempts by producers to escape from the often uncomfortable, but wholesome and beneficial, effect of market discipline imposed on them by consumer sovereignty. Frederic Bastiat (1801-1850) described such governmental interventions in the marketplace as "legalized theft" because, through the dictates of civil rulers, they help some citizens at the expense of others.

All of the above actions are defended by the special-interest groups who benefit as being fair and beneficial to consumers. When viewed through economic analysis, though, they are correctly seen as nothing more than special-interest efforts to raise the incomes of those who are protected or helped by the civil power to escape the dreaded and impartial sovereignty exerted by consumers in the competitive marketplace. For some years this writer wrote a syndicated newspaper column with the byline "The competitive market is the workingman's best friend." That is a true statement which has universal application. Everyone benefits in the long run when the civil authorities refuse to bow to special-interest pressures, but instead allow consumers to impose their natural sovereignty in the competitive marketplace.

Licensing laws are especially harmful to the interests of low-income people because such laws raise the incomes of licensed practitioners by severely limiting the entry of other would-be practitioners to the protected professions, and an influx of new practitioners would result in lower fees being charged to consumers. Thus, people in the licensed professions, through coercive government intervention, are able to impose higher prices on the general public because the public then has fewer alternatives to choose from. To confuse the matter and to make an otherwise simple-to-understand economic issue more difficult to grasp, special-interest groups often gain the support of the news media to tout the fallacy that licensed professions "protect the public from quacks." In reality the drive for licensing laws always comes from within the professional groups whose incomes are raised by imposing licensing laws.

All of the above-mentioned attempts to escape from the impartial effect of consumer sovereignty on producers can be successful only to the extent that the civil authorities can be induced to bestow special favors on the special-interest groups involved. Even the largest and most powerful corporations can quickly be brought to heel through the decisions of consumers to buy or not to buy, even though each individual consumer might be completely unaware of the buying decisions of others. This emphasizes a truth that is often overlooked: a long-term monopoly can only exist with the approval and protection of civil government.

Can this really be so? Look at an example from recent history: In the 1970s the officials of General Motors Corporation were convinced that the American public's growing favor for compact cars was only a temporary phenomenon that would soon pass. Retooling manufacturing plants is very expensive, so GM resisted market pressure to produce smaller cars. In spite of a massive advertising program by GM, sales plummeted. So much for the socialist/communist claim of "managed demand" by large corporations, which supposedly have the ability to manipulate consumer demand and spending through massive advertising! A giant corporation was thus pitted in the economic arena against millions of so-called "helpless" disorganized consumers.

The outcome of such a contest was certain from the very beginning! It could only go one way! If the top executives of GM in the 1970s had been better students of economic history, they would have remembered what had happened to Henry Ford, 40 years earlier when a similar contest was waged between the Ford Motor Company and consumers in the early 1930s. Mr. Ford had become a multi-millionaire through mass-producing the popular Ford Model "A," but consumer tastes were changing, and Mr. Ford – against clear signals from consumers that they wanted a new model automobile with different colors – became hard-headed and insisted on continued production of the old black Model "A" Ford. Henry Ford is reputed to have quipped, "The people can have any color car they want, as long as it is black!" Consumers made Mr. Ford a rich man as a result of his superior service to them, but he forgot that, in America, the consumer is king. His attitude shows how easy it is for successful producers to forget the crucially important con-cept of continued service to consumers and subservience to their demands in the marketplace!

What happened in the 1930's contest was this: Consum-ers either deferred making new purchases, or they turned to competing brands of autos made by firms who were more in tune with what consumers were demanding. It was during this period that General Motors, with its connection with E. I. DuPont and its new line of colored paints, started pro-ducing automobiles with different colors. Up until this time Ford had outsold General Motors, but GM quickly gained in market share as consumers left Ford Motor products and turned to GM. In 1932 Ford made a quick emergency change in tooling and produced the model "B" as a stop gap so it could tool up for a completely new model the following year. Then Ford soon came out with the revolutionary V-8 engine which made Ford automobiles the fastest things on wheels and helped win back lost customers.

Now, to fast-forward from the 1930s to the 1970s: As sales dropped, GM executives relearned the hard lesson that Henry Ford had experienced some 40 years before; and they, too, knuckled under to consumer demands and retooled their plants to produce the kind of autos consumers were demand-ing.

The point of this bit of "ancient" and recent economic history is this: Both Ford and GM had grown to their "powerful" positions in the auto industry by serving consumer wants and by catering to their idiosyncrasies – that is, their continued success is always dependent upon their willingness to readily submit to the impartial discipline exerted in the competitive marketplace by consumer sovereignty – regardless of how fickle producers might think consumers are. This is the only way in which small, weak companies are able to grow into large, "powerful" corporations that dominate certain markets. A giant corporation can exert "power" only so long as it remains properly subservient to the sovereign rule of consumers in the competitive free-market economy. In short, in a competitive marketplace, the real power does not rest with business firms, regardless of how "powerful" they might seem to be; it rests with the individual consumer who is free to spend his or her limited funds on the best bargains available. And this is as it should be, for in America the consumer is king.

CHAPTER 8

PROFIT: The Incentive to Serve, and the Reward for Serving Efficiently

> ...what profit hath he that laboured for the wind?
> – Ecclesiastes 5:16

Profit? ... Profit is probably the most misunderstood word in our vocabulary! Most people do not understand the economic need for profit; they do not understand what profit is, and they grossly overestimate the rate of profit that most business firms earn.

The need for profit in a free-enterprise economy is straightforward: The future is always uncertain; it therefore involves risk that business entrepreneurs are forced to undertake in their business activities. A person (the producer/entrepreneur) can be in a position to serve the needs of consumers tomorrow *only* if he is willing to put his capital and the labor of his mind at risk today while looking to the future.

Providing a product or service to one's fellowmen in a competitive market economy necessitates some degree of speculation by the entrepreneur who renders that service. Someone, for instance, first had to design a product and then speculate by investing vast outlays of cash to build a manufacturing plant; to purchase equipment and raw materials;

to hire and pay workers; to purchase marketing services. All of these steps had to be accomplished long before a refrigerator, automobile, suite of furniture, or suit of clothes could seemingly magically appear in a store showroom and be available whenever a consumer gets a sudden impulse to go shopping! Months, sometimes years, before you or I ever had any intention of buying anything in the marketplace, various competing entrepreneurs were busily engaged in the designing and making of products or services which they hoped we might some day be interested in purchasing.

The hope for profit exists naturally in a free society. It is one of the motivating forces that stimulates perceptive individuals to search society for existing or potential problems, to discover possible solutions for them, and then to offer whatever solutions consumers might find to their liking. Note the sequence of prior existence and events:

First, it is necessary to recognize that problems are pre-existent in society, though they might have gone unnoticed or been ignored previously by the public.

Second, it is helpful to understand that God blesses certain individuals with special abilities and skills to discover problems and work out various means to solve them. In the market economy, such persons are called entrepreneurs or "risk takers." (For biblical examples of God's bestowing of special gifts on individuals, see Bezaleel and Aholiab, who are mentioned in Ex. 31:1-11, and the spiritual gifts in the church mentioned in I Cor. 12.)

Third, an entrepreneurial-minded risk taker serves as a catalyst for discovering problems and working out possible solutions.

Fourth, the entrepreneur, at his or her own expense, offers a problem-solving solution at a price that the entrepreneur hopes fellow members of society might find attractive.

Finally, if the offered solution proves to be viable and cost-worthy to consumers, and if the problem-solving services are provided efficiently, then the risk-taking entrepreneur might be able to earn a profit from his labor and capital investment.

Thus, we see that the hope for profit is what provides entrepreneurs with the needed incentive to undergo risks to serve their fellowmen. It is the *hope* for profit that overcomes the risk element. Profit also serves as a handy guidepost for allocating the relatively scarce resources of land, labor, and capital efficiently. Realized profit is thus an economic reward bestowed by consumers for service that has been rendered efficiently in the marketplace. Service provided at a risk, and provided efficiently, produces a profit to the entrepreneur; while service provided at a risk, but provided inefficiently, results in a loss.

Without the hope of gaining a profit in the future, America could not be a nation of freely acting people because relatively few individuals would be willing to serve others in the marketplace if the hope for gain were absent. Civil rulers would then find it necessary to force people to work, just as in totalitarian political/economic systems where slave labor camps and other forms of forced labor are commonplace.

Note that it is not profit itself, but the *hope* of earning a profit, as a result of investing one's entrepreneurial effort and labor, which is necessary to make the wheels of industry turn in a free society. Profits can, in real life, be negative (losses) as well as positive. It is estimated, during normal times in any one year, that one-fourth of all business firms show an economic loss rather than a positive profit. During periods of recession or depression, the loss-rate will be much higher. Our American system is a profit-*and*-loss system, not just a system in which profits are guaranteed. For, in a free society, nothing can be guaranteed, except the right to be free and the right to try; lest freedom itself be lost. Entrepreneurs and producers can and do make mistakes in their planning and production processes; and, when they do, the mistake-related costs must be absorbed by the profit-seeking risk taker rather than being passed on to consumers, as they are in socialist societies.

In a socialistic economy (in which the civil government owns and controls the major means of economic production), or in a fascistic economy (in which the civil government regulates and controls privately owned business firms and can impose wage and price controls), mistake-related costs *can indeed* be passed on to consumers. But, in a free economy, people must be left free to fail as well as to succeed. This is what was meant by the statement made previously that "The competitive free-market is the workingman's best friend!" Oftentimes, if we keep an open mind, we learn more from our failures than from our successes. Mistakes, if evaluated properly, are simply building blocks to success. There is a learning curve to every undertaking, so free individuals must be allowed to experience the discipline and knowledge gained from making mistakes during the learning process.

What about losses? Well, negative profits (losses) serve as inescapable proof that the producer-entrepreneur (risk taker) somehow must have erred in judgment, that he actually failed to serve his fellowmen efficiently, and that he must therefore make needed adjustments if he is to succeed in the future. Owning and operating a successful business can be very rewarding financially as well as in personal fulfillment, but it is a calling that demands a high degree of self-discipline and responsibility to God in our service to others (employees, customers, and investors).

> Say ye to the righteous, that it shall be well . . .
> for they shall eat the fruit of their doings.
> – Isaiah 3:10

Realized profits, on the other hand, show that a desired product or service was in demand and that it was produced efficiently at a price that consumers were willing to pay. Implicit in this statement is the assumption that would-be competitors have the freedom to enter an industry in order to serve consumers. This is the general rule in the competitive American economy, except where the power of civil government is sometimes wielded to inhibit competition, such as government-granted monopolies and licensed professions.

Most people have a misconception about one aspect of profit. They wrongly think that a business firm's profit is paid for by the consumer in the form of higher prices – that the higher profit enjoyed by the business firm, the higher price that consumers must pay. Nothing could be further from the truth!

Profit earned in a competitive market economy is not paid for by the consumer, strange as that might seem! Earned profits are generated through cost-saving efficiencies (see below). A producer cannot artificially raise consumer prices by going through a mental calculation and then adding a certain amount of profit margin onto his costs of production. Why not? Because, in a competitive economy, consumers always have the pleasant option of purchasing from more efficient producers who offer products and services at lower prices. There is a *caveat* that must be mentioned here: Consumers who focus more on price savings will often have to settle for products of lower quality.

The mushrooming growth during the last two or three decades of the personal-computer industry provides a perfect example of *high-cost, low-profit* firms being squeezed out of business by *lower-cost, higher-profit* producers who offered better quality computers to consumers at lower prices. The same process occurred in the growth of some small retail department stores that started out in small towns but which developed into nationwide mass-merchandisers by more efficiently meeting consumer needs. The directing stimulus behind these success stories of consumer-benefitting companies is very simple: Consumers could care less what a particular producer's cost of production is; all that consumers are interested in is purchasing the best available product and service at the lowest price! This self-interest of consumers is not very pleasant for business firms that fail to efficiently meet consumer demands; but it is exceedingly healthy for consumers and for the economy as a whole, and especially for the management, employees, and investors of those firms that are successful.

It is true that, in the designing and planning stage, a producer will include a desired profit ratio in the estimated sale price of a good or service; but this is only a *mental* calculation to determine *beforehand* whether or not it would be wise for the producer to embark on the risk-taking project at all. In reality, an entrepreneur or merchant cannot arbitrarily make consumers pay even one penny more for a product than they are already willing to pay because of economic forces that are at work in the marketplace. No, the producer can never forget that, in a competitive market, consumers usually have other sources of supply and other alternatives open to them. Therefore, the producer's problem boils down to this: He can only *estimate* a price that he *hopes* enough consumers might be willing to pay for his product at some distant point in the future which will allow him to recoup all of his costs, plus a profit!

This is where the need for good market research comes into play *prior* to actual production. The entrepreneur/producer cannot be absolutely sure that the public will welcome with warm hearts the product he is planning to bring to the market. Nor can he unilaterally demand what consumers *must* pay for it. He can only engage in his pre-production planning and then produce an attractive product that he hopes will have enough consumer appeal to recoup his sunk costs. At this point, his only option is to offer his product at a *tentative* asking-price and wait to see how consumers will react.

If consumers react favorably to the producer's tentative asking price, then perhaps he will be able to recoup his costs of production and a profit as well; but, if consumers react negatively to the price tag, then thinner profits or losses will be the sure result!

How does all the planning and production come about? It works like this: The entrepreneur/producer starts by designing a proposed product and then estimating a future selling price for it at the point of sale, which might be weeks, months, or possibly even years in advance. Then he calculates *backwards* from the point of sale to the present time and starts counting up his various costs of production: labor; capital investment in buildings and machinery; utilities such as electric, gas, and water; supplies; outside advisors; interest on borrowed capital; and many other costs like licensing fees, etc. Then he compares his total cost of production against the estimated total sales volume at the estimated price he hopes consumers might be willing to pay.

Note the complete absence of coercion in the free-market process. The challenge that the entrepreneur/producer must face in his planning and pre-production activities is this: He must arrange, rearrange, and keep on rearranging his production process and his cost inputs until he can successfully reduce his costs below his expected income from sales so that he can serve consumers' wants efficiently and profitably. If he cannot do this in the planning stage, the product will never be brought to market.

The fact that some products are actually manufactured and then sold later at "fire sale" prices only serves to indicate one or two possibilities: Either the entrepreneur/producer miscalculated somewhere in his cost estimations and market research; or consumers changed their minds, in the mean time, about what they wanted or were willing to pay because of some unforeseen eventuality. Remember that weeks, months, or even years can take place before a planned product is actually brought to market.

Here is a current example: Right now, as this is being written, producers have been working for some years in developing fuel-cell power plants. Their hope is that their efficient fuel-cell technology will be used to power automobiles, home electric generating plants, and many other uses – all without the use of petroleum, and all power produced without polluting the atmosphere. If successful, this new technology will be revolutionary! It will make life better and do so at lower costs to consumers; and the potential profits to successful producers will be very great! Of course, if the new technology is not perfected and brought to market at prices that consumers are willing to pay, then the losses will be horrendous!

As we can see, in a competitive market economy, consumers are the ones who always have the last authoritative word. It is the consumer who ultimately has the ability to say "yea or nay" to the small or grandiose plans of producers. It is the consumer whose decisions determine who will earn profits at the point of sale, or who must suffer losses. It is for this very practical reason that profits cannot be added onto the price that consumers pay in a free-market economy. Thus, profits seemingly magically appear where only costs existed before.

Profits come out of no one's pocket in a free-market economy. They are actually *created* through good entrepreneurial planning and cost-saving efficiencies during the process of production. Thus, profits are willingly, though unknowingly, bestowed by consumers only onto those producers who serve consumer interests efficiently. Profits, in a truly competitive marketplace, are consistently earned only by efficient producers who are able to provide, at their own risk, a needed service to consumers. "Service, at a risk, in the hope of profit," is the mutually-beneficial ethical theme that is successfully followed by enlightened employer-employee teams in a free-market economy.

> Cast thy bread upon the waters: for thou shalt find it after many days.
> . . . Fear God, and keep his commandments: for this is the whole duty of man.
> – Ecclesiastes 11:1 & 12:13

CHAPTER 9

HOW FREEDOM IS LOST

The wicked shall be turned into hell,
and all the nations that forget God.
— Psalm 9:17

We have seen in previous chapters that:

1. Man has a *right* to be free and self-responsible because he is created in the very image and likeness of God (Gen. 1:26).

2. Man has a *duty* to preserve his freedom so he can retain his self-responsibility to his Creator (Ex. 8:1).

3. The biblical role of civil government is simply to maintain law and order so man's freedom and self-responsibility can be maximized (I Tim. 2:1-2).

4. A consistent out-working of the Christian or biblical view of man will naturally lead to a peaceable, voluntary society.

Now we want to consider the important question "How is freedom lost?"

Sometimes people lose their freedom by having liberty forcibly wrested from them by foreign conquerors. But usually freedom is lost when a free people voluntarily relinquish duties and responsibilities they consider onerous or surrender liberty for the illusion of security (promised by demagogic politicians). Once a people hand over their responsibilities to someone else, like the civil government, it is never long until their corresponding freedoms are also lost.

Freedom and responsibility are like a two-sided coin. If we pick up the coin of "Liberty" and turn it over, the other side will say "Responsibility." If we recognize the inevitable process of how freedom is lost—first willingly giving up responsibility, and then suffering the loss of corresponding liberty—it is easy to understand how liberty can be protected and preserved. The simple solution to preserving liberty is for a free people to tenaciously guard and cherish their individual responsibilities, for in doing so they will find the only solution to preserving their God-given freedom. With this important thought in mind, we share two pertinent verses from the Bible with you:

Eat thou not the bread of him that hath an evil eye,
neither desire thou his dainty meats:
For as he thinketh in his heart, so is he:
Eat and drink, saith he to thee; but his heart is not with thee.
– Proverbs 23:6-7

Now the Lord is that Spirit:
and where the Spirit of the Lord is,
there is liberty.
– II Corinthians 3:17

INDEX

SCRIPTURE INDEX
(Page references in parentheses)